SandCastle™

First Sounds

Brandi and Brent

Mary Elizabeth Salzmann

Consulting Editor, Diane Craig, M.A./Reading Specialist

ABDO
Publishing Company

Published by ABDO Publishing Company, 4940 Viking Drive, Edina, Minnesota 55435.

Printed in the United States.

Credits
Edited by: Pam Price
Curriculum Coordinator: Nancy Tuminelly
Cover and Interior Design and Production: Mighty Media
Child Photography: Steven Wewerka, Wewerka Photography
Photo Credits: AbleStock, Corbis Images, Kelly Doudna, Stockbyte

Library of Congress Cataloging-in-Publication Data

Salzmann, Mary Elizabeth, 1968-
    Brandi and Brent / Mary Elizabeth Salzmann.
        p. cm. -- (First sounds)
    ISBN 1-59679-130-6 (hardcover)
    ISBN 1-59679-131-4 (paperback)
        1. English language--Consonants--Juvenile literature. I. Title. II. Series.

PE1159 .S+
428.1--dc22

2004059628

SandCastle™ books are created by a professional team of educators, reading specialists, and content developers around five essential components that include phonemic awareness, phonics, vocabulary, text comprehension, and fluency. All books are written, reviewed, and leveled for guided reading, early intervention reading, and Accelerated Reader® programs and designed for use in shared, guided, and independent reading and writing activities to support a balanced approach to literacy instruction.

Let Us Know

After reading the book, SandCastle would like you to tell us your stories about reading. What is your favorite page? Was there something hard that you needed help with? Share the ups and downs of learning to read. We want to hear from you! To get posted on the ABDO Publishing Company Web site, send us e-mail at:

sandcastle@abdopub.com

SandCastle Level: Emerging

A B C D E F G H
I J K L M N O P Q
R S T U V W X Y Z

a b c d e f g h
i j k l m n o p q
r s t u v w x y z

Brandi

Brent

bread

broom

brush

brownie

bride

We like the .

We like the .

We like the .

We like the  .

We like the .

Brandi has bread.

Brent has brownies.

Brandi and Brent like bread and brownies.

Which of these pictures begin with br?

More words that begin with br

braid

breakfast

brick

bridge

broken

brook

brother

brown

About SandCastle™

A professional team of educators, reading specialists, and content developers created the SandCastle™ series to support young readers as they develop reading skills and strategies and increase their general knowledge. The SandCastle™ series has four levels that correspond to early literacy development in young children. The levels are provided to help teachers and parents select the appropriate books for young readers.

Emerging Readers
(no flags)

Beginning Readers
(1 flag)

Transitional Readers
(2 flags)

Fluent Readers
(3 flags)

These levels are meant only as a guide. All levels are subject to change.

ABDO
Publishing Company

To see a complete list of SandCastle™ books and other nonfiction titles from ABDO Publishing Company, visit **www.abdopub.com** or contact us at:
4940 Viking Drive, Edina, Minnesota 55435 • 1-800-800-1312 • fax: 1-952-831-1632